4

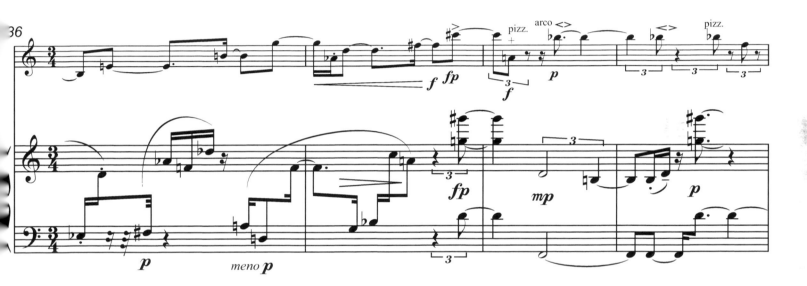

6

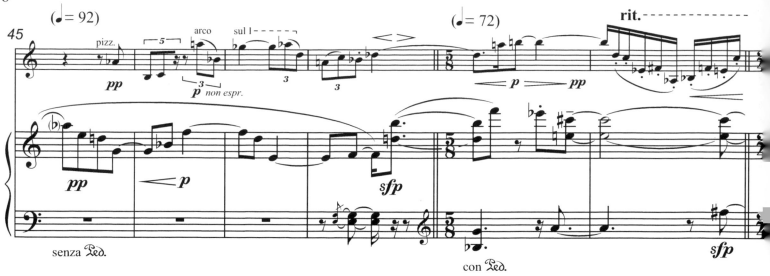

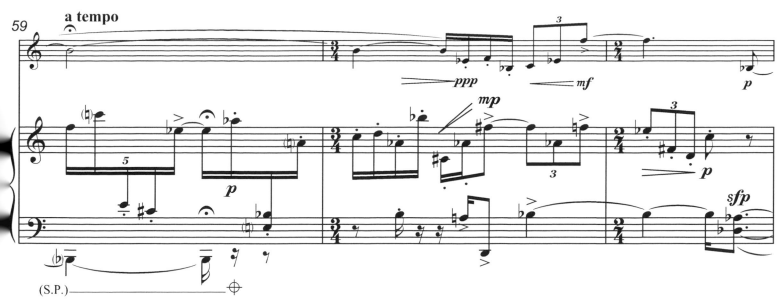

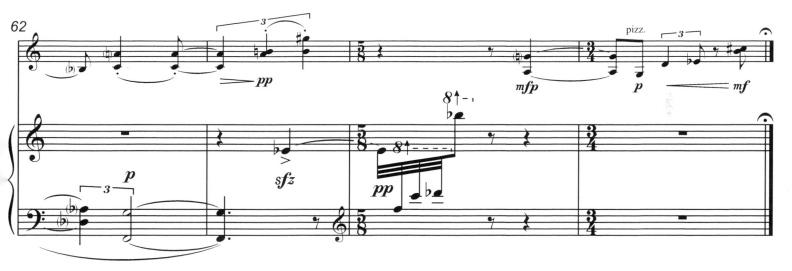

segue

8

II Variations: Moderato (♩. = ca. 88)

VIOLIN
Edited by Philip Ficsor

for John Verrall

Pastorale

WILLIAM BOLCOM
(1962)

I Allegretto grazioso ($\quarternote$ = 72)

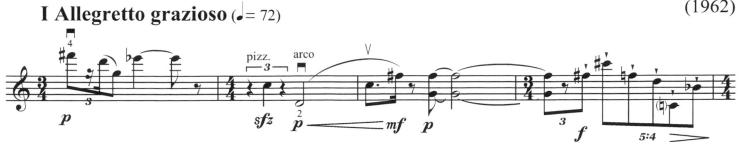

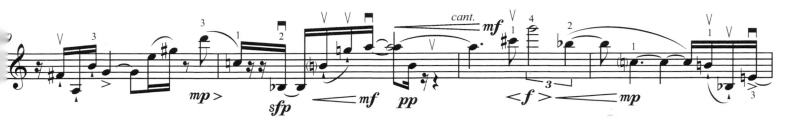

VIOLIN

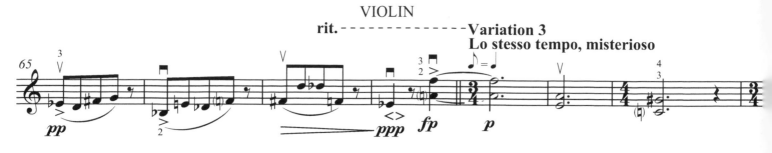

III Coda - Adagio espressivo (♩ = 69-84)

April 28, 1962

VIOLIN

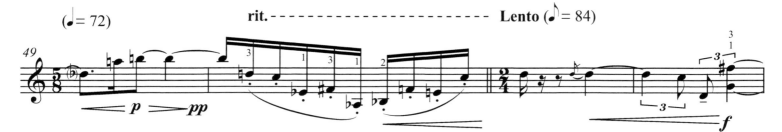

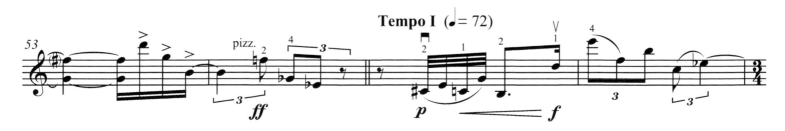

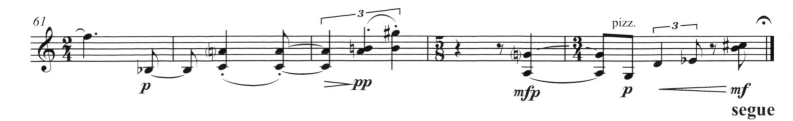

segue

Variation 1

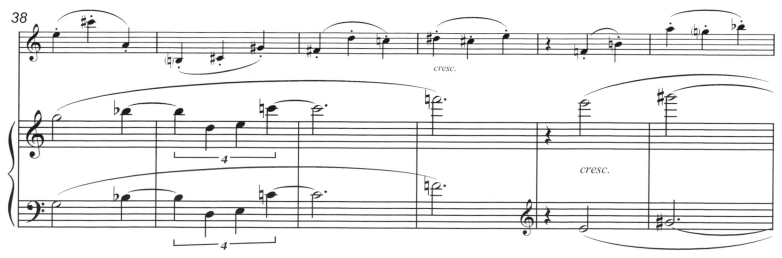

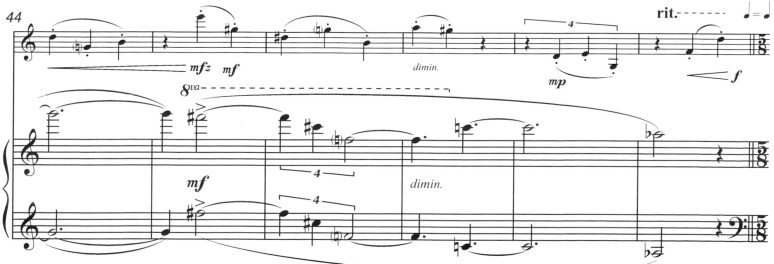

10

Variation 2

50 **Lo stesso tempo**

54

59

64

Ped.

Variation 3   Lo stesso tempo, *misterioso*

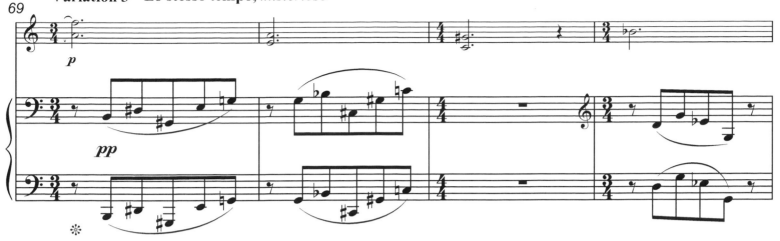

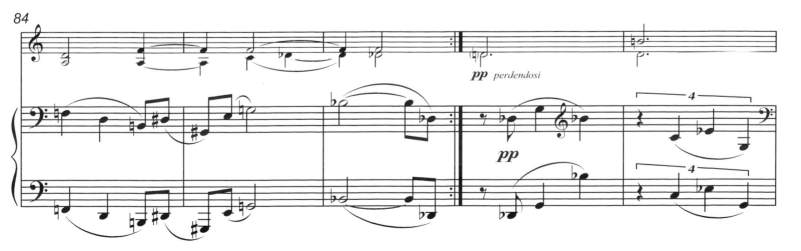

89

94

segue

III Coda - Adagio espressivo (♪ = 69-84)

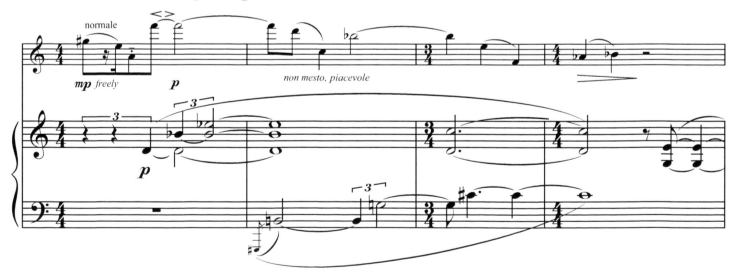

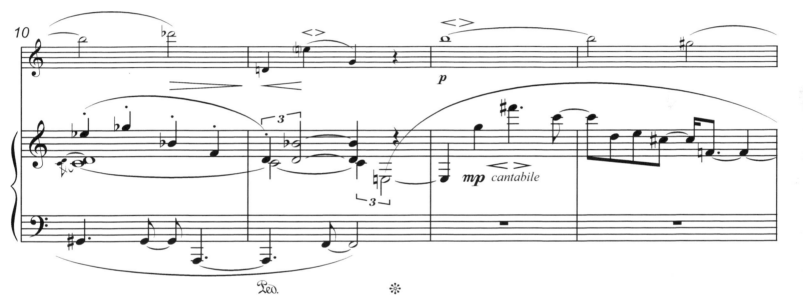

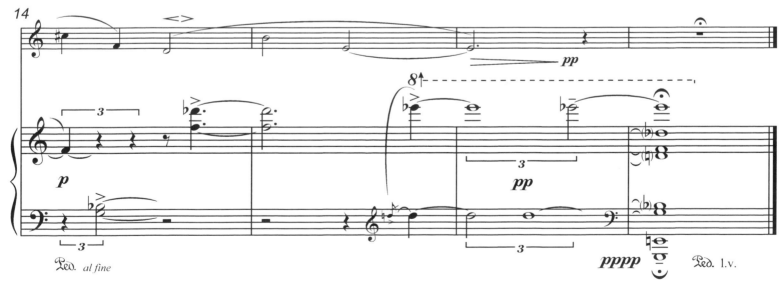

April 28, 1962

NOTE

Pastorale was first performed by John Verrall, Violin, and Emmanuel Zetlin, Piano in 1962.
It is dedicated to Mr. Verrall, a composition teacher of Mr. Bolcom.

NB:

1. Accidentals apply only throughout a beamed group.

2. There are slight differences between the violinist's part and that part in the score. What is in the score represents the composer's intentions . He approves, with thanks, the editorial suggestions made in the violin part by Philip Ficsor.